BENJAMIN FRANKLIN

The Life of a Printer, Scientist, and Revolutionary

THE HISTORY HOUR

D1602710

HISTORY

CONTENTS

"We are all born ignorant, but one must work hard to remain stupid."

— BENJAMIN FRANKLIN

❧ I ❧
INTRODUCTION

❦

Benjamin Franklin is one of the most famous names in American history.

> *While he is mainly known for flying a kite during a*
> *thunderstorm and being one of the 56 Founding*
> *Fathers of the United States of America, he is also*
> *known as being the one to say, "Early to bed, early*
> *to rise makes a man healthy, wealthy, and wise."*

But there is a lot more to this man. Not only was Benjamin Franklin a son, brother, husband, and scientist, he was also one of the most famous men during his time. Not only was he very popular and highly respected in the American colonies, which would become the United States of America in his later life, but he was also highly respected in other countries in the world, such as England and France, at least during some periods of his life.

๛

Throughout his life, Benjamin Franklin was determined and hard-working. He was also highly intelligent and a very generous and compassionate human being, who often woke up early and would ask himself what good he could accomplish that day. He is a man who had many excellent chapters in his life. This work will be a focus of all the pieces in Benjamin Franklin's life that helped make him the Benjamin Franklin most people know and love to this day.

❧ II ❧
EARLY LIFE

"Tell me, and I forget; teach me, and I may remember; involve me, and I learn."

— BENJAMIN FRANKLIN

THE CHILDHOOD OF BENJAMIN FRANKLIN

❧

B enjamin Franklin was born on January 17, 1706, to Josiah and Abiah Franklin in Boston. He was the 15th out of 17 children. His father had immigrated from England in 1682. His mother was the daughter of one of New England's first settlers, Peter Folger. While the Franklin family was not rich, they did well for themselves. Josiah had his own candle and soap making business. His mother kept busy in the home. Not only did she care for her all her young children, but she also cleaned, cooked, sung psalms, spin wool, kept her husband's bank books, wove cloth, sew and taught the children prayers.

❧

Religion was a vital piece in the Franklin household. Benjamin was raised in a Puritan home and spent many Sundays and Thursdays listening to Cotton Mather as a child. The family would sit in church for up to four hours. The

Puritans had strict rules in the church, and one was that you had to sit up straight and be quiet. On top of this, they also had to follow other rules, such as the color of clothing and what type of activities the church could do on Sundays.

❧

As a child, Benjamin spent a lot of time alone, and he did not particularly get along with any of his brothers and sisters. During his time alone, he would teach himself specific life skills, such as learning how to swim. He was able to learn these skills by reading books. Benjamin Franklin loved to read books. He would save every penny he could to buy books and borrow from friends.

❧

Education was also crucial in the Franklin household. However, there was not a lot of formal education. But because Josiah had dreams that Benjamin would one day become a Clergyman, Benjamin was enrolled in the Boston Grammar School when he was around eight years old. However, Benjamin's time at the Boston Grammar School was short lived as a year later, Josiah took Ben out of the school. Many historians continue to wonder why Josiah pulled Benjamin out because he was at the top of his class. Some believe that the reason was money while others think that Josiah simply gave up on the idea of Benjamin becoming a Clergyman. Other historians feel that Josiah believed he could get a better education elsewhere. Whatever the reason was, Benjamin was later enrolled in Mr. Brownell's School for Writing and Arithmetic.

❧

Later in his life, Benjamin wrote that he excelled in writing but struggled in arithmetic. He was taken out of Mr. Brownell's School for Writing and Arithmetic a year later. This would be the end of Benjamin's formal education. Instead, his father believed that he could start learning at home and in his candle and soap business. While Benjamin did not enjoy making candles, he did enjoy listening in on the political and life advice and opinions his father would often give the town people. They would usually come to Josiah while the family was sitting down at the dinner table. Josiah would allow Benjamin to stay at the table to listen in and enrich his mind. Later in life, Benjamin wrote that he would become so interested in the conversation that he would forget to eat.

BEN FRANKLIN: THE
BEGINNING PIECES

ॐ

When Benjamin was twelve years old, his father decided to make him an apprentice at his brother, James' printing press. This was one of the first steps in Ben's young life that would lead him down his life's path. Benjamin was in charge of setting the letters for the printer along with selling the newspapers in the town. However, this job did not satisfy Benjamin Franklin. Instead, Benjamin had dreams about wanting to write for the newspaper and not just continue with the busy work. However, Benjamin knew his brother would object to the thought of Benjamin writing for the newspaper, which was called, *The Courant*. Therefore, one day Benjamin left an anonymous article under the door of his brother's print house. But, instead of signing his name, he signed it as Silence Dogood. James liked the Dogood letters so much that he published all of them, which he received from April to October of 1722. Unfortunately, the letters did not sit well with the Assembly, and they asked James to reveal the writer. When James refused, mostly because he did not know who the real author was, he was placed in jail for two weeks, which left Benjamin in charge of the printing business. When James was released, he was banned from printing the newspaper, so Benjamin continued for a while. However, he grew tired of his brother's abuse and decided to take the opportunity to escape from the apprentice contract he had signed three years earlier, at twelve years old.

৩৯৫৩

But because James had gone around Boston and told other printers not to hire Benjamin, he was unable to get another printing job in Boston. Therefore, Ben snuck out of his brother's house in 1723, at sixteen years old, and onto a ship headed to New York City. It did not take Benjamin long to realize he was not going to find a printing job in New York City. So, with the advice of New York City printers, he headed to the biggest city in the American colonies, Philadelphia.

৩৯৫৩

Once in Philadelphia, Franklin found a job with Samuel Keimer. It was not too much longer the governor of Pennsylvania went to see Franklin. He ended up offering Franklin a way to set up his own printing business. Benjamin Franklin agreed, and the governor sent him to London for supplies. However, once Benjamin landed in London, he realized he was stranded. Governor Sir William Keith did not send along any letters of credit or money. Benjamin was now penniless, homeless, and in a foreign country. So, he did the only thing he could - find a printing job. Eventually, Franklin was hired at Palmers. He worked there for a year and a half until

9

Thomas Denham paid for Benjamin's trip back to Philadelphia. Once Benjamin stepped foot back on American soil, he knew more than any other printer in Pennsylvania. Within a year after being back, Benjamin opened his own printing business.

❧ III ❧
THE BEGINNING OF A
MASTER MIND

"I am for doing good to the poor, but...I think the best way of doing good to the poor, is not making them easy in poverty but leading or driving them out of it. I observed...that the more public provisions were made for the poor, the less they provided for themselves, and of course became poorer. And, on the contrary, the less was done for them, the more they did for themselves, and became richer."

— BENJAMIN FRANKLIN

THE START OF FREEDOM

❧

Because of an essay Benjamin Franklin wrote in Pennsylvania titled, "***The Nature and Necessity of a Paper Currency,***" Franklin became the official printer in the colony. Six years later, in 1736, Benjamin Franklin would become the official printer for paper currency in New Jersey.

❧

However, even holding one of the most prestigious printing jobs in Colonial America was not Benjamin's most significant business accomplishment. His greatest business accomplishment would be the *Poor Richard's Almanac*. The first one was printed under the name Richard Saunders on December 19, 1732. For the next 25 years, the *Poor Richard's Almanac* would be published annually. The publication held a variety of information, such as weather predictions, demographics, a calendar, poems, trivia, proverbs, recipes, and other interesting facts and information. Very quickly, the almanac became the most read material in the American colonies, especially for those who could not afford books. About 10,000 copies of the *Poor Richard's Almanac* were printed annually.

⚜

With the success of the *Poor Richard's Almanac* and his other business ventures, Benjamin Franklin had become very wealthy and famous. But Benjamin knew he wanted to do other things in his life. So, in 1748, he hired a partner to take care of the daily printing tasks. With David Hall employed, Franklin was able to engage in experiments and public projects. Hall and Franklin would remain printing business partners until 1766 when Franklin would sell the business to Hall.

⚜

One of Benjamin Franklin's favorite things to do was writing. During his life, he not only became one of the best printers in Colonial America but also became a well-known writer around the globe. Not only did he write thousands of letters to various people, including family, friends, and business associates, but he also wrote and published pamphlets, almanacs, articles, and essays.

⚜

Other than the *Poor Richard's Almanac*, one of Franklin's most well-known works was Father Abraham and "The Way to Wealth." Father Abraham was created when Benjamin Franklin was gathering all the articles in the Almanac about investing money. Through these articles, Benjamin wrote a story about Father Abraham, who had been an avid reader of the *Poor Richard's Almanac* for 25 years. The story was published in the 1758 almanac and was an immediate hit with its readers. Even though the story was ironic, it was also humorous and had its readers laughing.

❧

Benjamin also spent many nights writing his autobiography. He had started in the late 1760s, however, would never be able to finish it. When the American Revolutionary War began, he had to put the autobiography aside, and it was nearly lost. After retirement, he did work on it but very little. When he died, the book only went as far as 1757. But, even though it is unfinished, Benjamin Franklin's autobiography is a famous work in American literature.

✻ IV ✻
FAMILY LIFE WITH BENJAMIN FRANKLIN

"Half a truth is often a great lie."

— BENJAMIN FRANKLIN

A RELATIONSHIP OF TWO
COLONIALS

❦

Benjamin Franklin met his future wife, Deborah Read, when he first got to Philadelphia. He ended up boarding with Deborah and her parents. They quickly fell in love but had a rough courtship. While Franklin was stuck in England for eighteen months, Deborah married John Rogers, who was a potter in Philadelphia. Unfortunately, Deborah and John's happy marriage was short-lived. Not only did John spend money freely and occur a significant amount of debt, but there was also a rumor that he had a wife in England. Deborah could not take anymore heartache from John, so she went back to her mother's house, and John headed to the West Indies.

❦

Around the same time that John sailed off, Franklin returned to the colonies. Benjamin was heartbroken to hear of their marriage as now he could not marry Deborah. However, it was not too much longer when rumors started circulating that John had died at sea. Both Deborah and Benjamin hoped these rumors were true.

> *While Benjamin stated, "I took her to wife on September 1, 1730," they did not record their marriage to the church.*

Instead, Benjamin and Deborah had a common law marriage. Deborah moved in with Benjamin and started referring to herself as Mrs. Benjamin Franklin. A common law marriage was an acceptable marriage in the 1700s. Deborah and Benjamin believed this was the best marriage for them because they did not truly know if John was dead or if it was just a rumor. If John was not dead, Deborah was not free to marry. If Deborah and Benjamin recorded their marriage to the church and John returned, both Benjamin and Deborah would be charged with bigamy. This was a severe crime in Colonial America, and it was publishable by life imprisonment and 39 lashes.

୧୨୫

Through Benjamin Franklin's marriage, you can read how much he loved and cared for Deborah, even if he was not always around. During their marriage, and for the rest of Benjamin Franklin's life, Benjamin would only talk and write about his wife's positive points. He never talked ill of her or would discuss her flaws, even though many other people Benjamin spoke and wrote to knew about her shortcomings. He never wrote of any frustrations he had towards Deborah.

> *In fact, he once wrote that Deborah was "a good and faithful helpmate." He further wrote that*

> Deborah *"cheerfully attended me in my business,*
> *folding and stitching pamphlets, tending shop,*
> *purchasing old linen rags for the papers makers,*
> *etc., etc."*

❧

However, just because Benjamin and Deborah love each other and spoke well of one another, does not mean Benjamin and Deborah had a perfect marriage. As Benjamin Franklin started to make his mark in the American colonial world as a printer, writer, scientist, and statesman; the couple began to drift apart. The more and more Benjamin was gone, spending time with the public and not his wife, Deborah became more and more jealous and lonely.

> *"All the world claims the privilege of troubling my*
> *Pappy." Deborah once told a good friend.*

Pappy was Deborah's nickname for Benjamin.

❧

As Benjamin Franklin's fame began to reach increasing heights around the world, he started traveling abroad. In 1757, he left for England. No matter how much Deborah would plead with her husband to return, Benjamin would not return home. Benjamin did not even return home when his wife suffered a severe stroke, leaving her with slurred speech and poor memory, in 1768-1769. Benjamin Franklin found out about his wife's death in February of 1775, through the *Pennsylvania Gazette*, which read, "On Monday, the 19th of December, died Mrs. Deborah Franklin, wife of Dr. Franklin." While this may make Benjamin seem like he had given up on his marriage to Deborah, the opposite is proven in Benjamin's writings after his wife's death.

> He stated, "I have lost my old and faithful companion...and I every day become more sensible of the great loss which cannot be repaired."

This is proof that Benjamin still loved and cherished Deborah, as he always had.

FATHER AND GRANDFATHER

❧

Benjamin Franklin's first born son was named William "Billy" Franklin. No one is really sure when William was born but know that he was born either late 1730 or early 1731. Of course, many people around Philadelphia talked and discussed rumors about Benjamin Franklin's illegitimate son. Many people, including historians today, wondered who William's mother was. To most people, there were only two choices. The first choice was William was Deborah's son, conceived before their common law marriage. However, the increasing mistreatment that Deborah gave to William often makes people believe this was not the case. The second choice was another woman, who many believed was a servant who worked in the Franklin household named Barbara, was William's mother.

❧

While we never get any definitive answer from anyone on who William's mother is, later in his life, Benjamin Franklin wrote that William was a product of lust. This lust, Benjamin would explain, was an action he was unable to control. Even so, Benjamin loved William, just as he loved his other two children, and took full responsibility for being William's father. Deborah agreed to raise William as her own, and while she did, she gave him little affection compared to her other two children. And the older William would get, the more and more Deborah would openly discuss and show her dislike for William. Thankfully for William, he received great love and attention from Benjamin. While their love and adoration for each other would last the rest of their lives, they would not always be on the best terms, especially after the American Revolution.

Because of King George III's influence over William in 1757, which was when William followed his father to England, William remained loyal to the king during the American Revolution. During America's fight for independence, it was father against son. Benjamin had fought hard to save his life, lives of the other Founding Fathers, and gain America's independence. William did not believe America could win the war or govern themselves and fought against the American cause. After the American Revolution, the two wrote to each other. These letters would prove that they still loved and cared for each other but would not be able to get over their emotions caused by their different sides during the American Revolution.

William, who was living in London, wrote to his father:

> *"How I desire to revive that affectionate intercourse*
> *and connection which till the commencement of*
> *the late troubles had been the pride and happiness*
> *of my life. You must know I acted from a strong*
> *sense of what I conceived my duty to my king and*
> *my country. I verily believe if that werethe same*
> *circumstances to occur tomorrow, my conduct*
> *would be exactly similar...All this, however, his*
> *history...My fondest hope is now to resume our*
> *relationship as it was before."*

࿇

In response to his son's letter, Benjamin wrote:

> *"Nothing has ever hurt me so much and affected me*
> *with such keen sensations as to find myself*
> *deserted in my old age by my own son. And not*
> *only deserted, but to find him taking up arms*
> *against me in a cause where in my good fame,*
> *fortune, and life were all at stake... There are*
> *natural duties which proceed political ones, and*
> *cannot be extinguished by them...This is a*
> *disagreeable subject. I drop it...I shall be glad to*
> *see you when convenient, but would not have you*
> *come here at present."*

࿇

When Benjamin wrote this response to William, he was in France and still angry over the betrayal of his firstborn son.

But in 1785, when Benjamin was heading back to America from France, he met up with William in England. However, it was not the greatest father and son reunion. Benjamin could not let go of the anger he felt towards William. Furthermore, William could sense his father's hostility, which made him feel awkward and uncomfortable. This would be the last time William and Benjamin would see each other as nothing was resolved at their meeting.

William would not be Benjamin Franklin's only son but would be his only son to live to adulthood. In 1732, Benjamin and his wife welcomed Francis Folger. Francis contracted smallpox and passed away at four years old, so not much is known of his life. What historians do know is that he loved to follow his father at the printing business. It is also well known that Benjamin never got over the death of little Francis. Until his dying day, Benjamin would cry for his second born son. He would wonder what would have become of his Francis. Whenever he saw a young boy, his mind would think of the young son he lost.

> *"I always thought he would be the best of my children."*

Benjamin Franklin would write of Francis near the end of his life, fifty years after the loss.

> *"To this day, I cannot think of him without a sigh."*

In 1743, Benjamin and Deborah would welcome another child into their lives. This time, they would welcome a daughter, whom they would name Sarah. However, she was usually called by her nickname of Sally. With William a teenager and Francis already passed, Sally often felt as though she was an only child.

> *Like with his other two children, Benjamin adored*
> *his daughter. He proudly wrote about Sally,*
> *stating she "...is the greatest lover of her books*
> *and school."*

Because Sally's true love was music, Benjamin sent her a harpsichord when he was living in England. Upon his return to America, the father and daughter would spend some of their most treasured time making music. Sally would play the harpsichord as Benjamin would play the glass harmonica, an instrument that he developed.

๑๕๗

Sally married a man by the name of Richard Bache in 1767, while Benjamin was in England. Sally and Richard would continue to live in the Franklin household, where they would raise their seven children. Sally would also care for her father in his old age, especially the last four to five years of his life.

๑๕๗

Benjamin could not think of a better way to live out his remaining years than living with his daughter, son-in-law, and his grandchildren, or his little prattlers, as he would call them.

He wrote of Benny, Willy, Betsy, Louis, Deborah, Richard, and little Sarah, "I am now in the bosom of my family, and find a batch of new babies who cling about the knees of their grandpapa, and afford me great pleasure."

❧ V ❧

A KITE, ELECTRICITY, AND INVENTIONS

"If a man empties his purse into his head no one can take it away from him. An investment in knowledge always pays the best interest."

— BENJAMIN FRANKLIN

BEGINNING STAGES

❦

A s a child, Benjamin's mind was always on the go. He would be performing a daily activity, such as swimming, and have an idea he would have to experiment with. For example, one day Benjamin decided to go for a swim as he was flying his kite. He laid down on his back in the water, held the stick, and let the kite pull him along the surface of the water. Today, this is considered Benjamin Franklin's first scientific experiment. Later in his life, he wanted to expand this experiment to the English Channel. However, he realized that it would be much better and safer to use a boat or a ship instead of test his little experiment.

❦

Another scientific childhood activity was creating his own magic square of squares. This activity was forming a square filled with numbers so that the sum of every vertical, horizontal, and diagonal row was equal. This activity would follow

Benjamin into adulthood when he would often create a magic square of squares when he was bored or has some downtime.

⚜

Throughout his childhood and into adulthood, Benjamin Franklin continued to observe, explore, and examine everything around him. Franklin wondered how ants were always able to find their way into his molasses jar. He had even moved the jar, and every time the ants would find their way. Through his various experiments with the molasses jar and ants, Benjamin believed that ants have their own language, and when one ant finds out about something, such as food, it goes back to the colony to inform the other ants.

AND ELECTRIFIED LIFE

❧

While Benjamin conducted several experiments, he is most well known for his experiments with electricity. In fact, electricity was one of Benjamin Franklin's favorite topics for experimentation. Furthermore, Benjamin would become famous when he was performing his electrical experiments.

He once wrote, "my house was continually full of persons who came to see the new wonders."

Often, the experiments Benjamin would perform in front of an audience, he had done many times. One such experiment was called the counterfeit spiders. In this experiment, Benjamin creates a life-like but fake spider out of a burned cork and linen thread. The cork was the body, and the linen thread was the legs of the fake spider. This counterfeit spider was then attached to a wire. The spider would then move and jump around when the wire was touched by a form of electricity, such as an electrical battery, which had been one of Benjamin Franklin's inventions. Benjamin always enjoyed this experiment because his audience would believe it was a real spider as it would move so fast and they would not be able to tell the difference.

❦

With each new experiment, Benjamin would record the steps and the process down and share them with his good friend, Peter Collinson. Peter thoroughly enjoyed reading about Benjamin's experiments and told Franklin they needed to be shared. Therefore, in 1751, Collinson gathered together all of the descriptions of Benjamin Franklin's experiments he had received and published them in a book. It would be this book, which was titled, *Experiments and Observations on Electricity*, that would make Benjamin Franklin a worldwide scientist.

❦

Nearly everyone has seen a painting of Benjamin Franklin and his son, William, flying a kite in a thunderstorm, waiting for lightning to strike. There are many versions of this painting and is Benjamin Franklin's most commonly discussed experiment.

❦

The great date occurred in June of 1752. It was this afternoon when Benjamin was watching for an intense thunderstorm that was supposed to roll through his area. By this time, Benjamin had come to the belief that lightning and electricity were the same. To test his theory, Benjamin made a kite out of silk instead of paper. The kite also had a miniature metal rod at its top. Benjamin had also attached a handkerchief at the end, so the person holding the kite would be better protected by an electrical shock. There was also a wire that went from the top of the metal rod and down. At the bottom end of the wire, a key was attached. This key, Benjamin believed, would be able to collect an electrical charge and start moving due to the charge. Benjamin's goal was to fly the kite in the eye of the storm. As the kite was flying in the storm, Benjamin touched the key. It was then he became very excited because he felt a very familiar electrical shock. In fact, it was the same type of electrical shock he felt when he would touch one of his invented electric batteries. However, unlike his other scientific experiments, he did not share this experiment with the scientific community right away. In fact, Benjamin did not even record the day or time of the experiment. Benjamin Franklin kept his findings of the kite experiment a secret for months. To this day, historians are not sure why he did this, but some suspect that it was because he knew what this type of finding could do in the scientific community, and he would be in the middle of it. Others feel that Franklin wanted to make sure that he had indeed discovered what he believed he discovered.

⚜

Benjamin Franklin's famous kite and lightning experiment led him to invent the lightning rod.

> *With this invention, Benjamin stated, "One should fix, at the highest parts, rods of iron, made sharp as a needle...and from the foot of these needles, a wire run down outside of the building and protecting them from lightning."*

DISCOVERIES OF ELECTRICITY

❧

T hrough all of his experimenting with electricity, Benjamin made several discoveries, which he noted. One of these notes was that both electricity and lightning make a noise when they explode. He also noted that they both give off light, can cause a fire, and can kill.

❧

In fact, that lightning and electricity could damage property or kill someone was one of the reasons why people were cautious about putting a lightning rod on the top of their homes. While some people did follow Benjamin Franklin's advice of the lightning rod after they read about it in the *Poor Richard's Almanac*, many people continued to feel it was too dangerous.

❧

Benjamin also developed the terms *"negative"* and *"positive"* when referring to an electrical charge. On top of this, he also discovered that some materials had better conditions than others, therefore, allowing electricity to pass through them easier. Through a previous experiment, before the famous kite experiment, Benjamin discovered that some materials, such as silk, would be insulators from an electrical shock.

☙❦☙

While most of Benjamin Franklin's scientific experiments and discoveries seem little or minor today, they were extremely important and valuable during Benjamin Franklin's life. In fact, they were so groundbreaking that The Royal Society awarded him the Copley Medal, which was England's highest honor for a scientist. On top of this, three highly esteemed universities, Oxford, Harvard, and Yale, awarded Benjamin Franklin with honorary degrees. This would be the reason why some people would start referring to Benjamin Franklin as Dr. Franklin. These honorary degrees were some of the most treasured materials that Benjamin Franklin ever received. Franklin was always a bit embarrassed that he only had two years of formal schooling. And, on top of that, while schooling was more informal than formal during Benjamin Franklin's time, it was not often that a person like Franklin, who had such little formal schooling, would become so highly respected in a field, especially the scientific community.

AN INVENTOR BEFORE HIS TIME

❧

Not only did Benjamin Franklin dive into scientific experiments, but he was also an inventor of many items. Along with the glass armonica, he also invented bifocals.

❧

Benjamin Franklin is well known for wearing glasses. While not all of his portrait paintings have him painted with glasses on, a couple do. And while people know he wore glasses, it is a little-known fact that from the 1780s until the end of his life, Benjamin Franklin wore one, if not the first pair, of bifocals. Benjamin wore glasses throughout most of his adult life, however, as time went on, he started to need two pairs of glasses. He needed one to see this close up and he needed a different pair so he could see things far away. This means that Benjamin Franklin was both near and far sided. Therefore, he had to carry two pairs of glasses. Eventually, Benjamin felt changing between the two pairs of glasses was impractical. He then brought both pairs of glasses to a glass shop, where he asked the owner to cut each pair of lenses in half. He then glued one half from each pair of glasses together to create new lenses. He was then able to either look through the top half of his glasses or the bottom half of his glasses to see what he needed to see better.

When discussing his bifocals, Benjamin stated, "I found this most convenient."

⚜

To continue his scientific experiments, especially the ones that focused on an electrical charge, Benjamin realized he needed a contraption to give himself enough of an electrical charge. Knowing the rubbing two items together could create friction, Benjamin realized he needed to invent something built off that idea. This was when he invented what he called the electrostatic machine. Basically, the machine was a very early version of an electrical generator. The contraption had a glass globe at the top, a wheel, and a piece of chamois skin. When the glass globe would rub against the chamois skin, a static electric charge would result. The electrical charge came from a bunch of knitting needles and was stored in a Leyden jar. Benjamin was thankful that this invention worked for his experiments. With this invention, Benjamin knew he would receive enough electricity for his experiments.

⚜

For his inventions, Benjamin did not always create an object. At one point, Benjamin tried to create an easier alphabet for the English language. This came about because he saw how poorly many people, especially women, spelled. Of course, during Benjamin's time, formal education was not as easy as it is today, and women simply received none to very little formal education. Because of the lack of formal education, people would write words simply by how they sounded. In his alphabet, Benjamin eliminated certain letters that did not match their sounds, such as q, x, and y. He also went on to create new letters that he felt would be necessary to help people spell better when they spelled by how a word sounded. Benjamin tested this newly formed alphabet on some of his friends when he wrote them letters. While some friends tried to write back the same way, it was challenging for everyone, including Benjamin Franklin, to let go of the alphabet they had known all their lives. Therefore, he set his invented alphabet aside and kept using the regular English alphabet. As Benjamin wrote that he could not "*uz a simplrverzun al hizlyf.*"

❧ VI ❧
OTHER PIECES OF
BENJAMIN FRANKLIN

"If you would know the value of money, go try to borrow some; for he that goes a-borrowing goes a-sorrowing."

— BENJAMIN FRANKLIN

A WELL-ROUNDED INDIVIDUAL

❧

Not only was Benjamin Franklin a scientist and inventor, but he also held many other pieces throughout his life. One of these pieces was starting a volunteer fire department in Philadelphia. He also helped build a hospital and worked on bettering formal education. While America was still the thirteen colonies, Franklin was its head postmaster. But, above all these puzzle pieces which helped develop Benjamin Franklin's life, he focused on becoming the best person he could be.

❧

Just like Thomas Jefferson and many other people during his time, Benjamin Franklin followed a strict daily schedule. Not only was this schedule to help him stay on task, but it was also so he could help himself in becoming perfect. Benjamin was in his late 20s when he decided he would try to become perfect. To achieve this goal, he came up with a list of thirteen rules to follow, which he wrote down and kept in a small notebook that he carried with him wherever he went. His theory to better himself with these thirteen rules was to work on one rule a week. Once week thirteen was up, he would start over. However, Benjamin eventually came to realize that perfection was impossible. Even so, he kept the little notebook with him for the rest of his life. He would not only carry it with him wherever he went, but he would also show people this notebook and explain the thirteen rules. Benjamin Franklin's thirteen rules were as follows:

1. Temperance. Eat not to dullness. Drink not to elevation.
2. Silence. Speak not but what may benefit others or yourself. Avoid trifling conversation.
3. Order. Let all things have their places. Let each part of your business have its time.
4. Resolution. Resolve to perform what you ought. Perform without fail what you resolve.
5. Frugality. Make no expense but to do good to others or yourself: i.e., waste nothing.
6. Industry. Lose no time. Be always employed in something useful.
7. Sincerity. Use no hurtful deceit. Think innocently and justly; and, if you speak, speak accordingly.
8. Justice. Wrong none, by doing injuries or omitting the benefits that are your own duty.
9. Moderation. Avoid extremes. Forbear resenting injuries so much as you think they deserve.
10. Tranquility. Be not disturbed at trifles, or at accidents, common or unavoidable.
11. Cleanliness. Tolerate to uncleanness in body, clothes, or habitation.

12. Chastity. Rarely use venery but for health or offspring.
13. Humility. Imitate Jesus and Socrates.

❦

One service that Benjamin Franklin continued throughout his life was community service. Benjamin always believed that the "best service to God, is doing good to man."

> *Therefore, one of the first questions Benjamin would ask himself in the morning was "What good shall I do today?"*

❦

This part of his day was so important to him that he wrote it into his daily schedule. Of the task, he once wrote:

❦

> *"I rose at five each morning, and addressed Powerful Goodness (Benjamin's name for God) with the same daily question: What good shall I do today? I then studied and planned my day until eight, worked until twelve, dined and overlooked my account book until two, worked again until six when I had supper, music, and conversation. At ten, I examined my day. What good had I done that day?"*

TO BETTER A COMMUNITY IN
THE EYES OF FRANKLIN

❧

I n 1736, Benjamin Franklin organized the Union Fire Company, which would basically be Philadelphia's first volunteer fire department. Benjamin got the idea from a club which had been started in London and formed to fight fires. Benjamin helped create a group of thirty men with the men appointing Benjamin Franklin as its first fire chief. All the men were not only trained in fighting fires but also rescuing people. Due to Benjamin's work within the fire department and their monthly meetings discussing fire prevention, the department became huge in numbers of volunteers.

❧

Another way Benjamin worked on the safety of his community was making the streets safer. The same year he established the fire department, he worked on getting the trash picked up from the roads and improved the street lights.

These lights had a hole at the top, so instead of having the smoke from the candle stay trapped in a globe, like the previous street lights, the smoke of the candle could escape through the hole. On top of this, Benjamin hired a group of individuals to be the lamplighters for the city. These men were in charge of lighting the candle at night and any maintenance.

§

One of Benjamin Franklin's goals in life was to develop better formal education for boys. Benjamin always regretted not getting enough formal education in his childhood, and he wanted better for the future generation. Therefore, in the late 1740s, Benjamin published the "***Proposals relating to the Education of Youth in Pennsylvania.***" This booklet explained Benjamin Franklin's plan for free education for boys in the colony. The plan would only cover boys ages eight to sixteen and did not include girls.

§

While some historians believe that girls were not included because it was simply not typical for girls to obtain a formal education during Benjamin's time, others have a different theory. While Benjamin Franklin was known to be a kind soul, he had a certain view of women that was a bit typical of his time. No matter how ahead of his time Benjamin was in his thinking with experiments and inventions, he believed women had a certain place, and they were not to be removed from that place. And this place, even in Benjamin Franklin's mind, was in the home, as he discussed when he wrote about his ideal female:

*"With the best natural disposition in the world, she
discovers daily the seeds and tokens of industry,
economy, and in short, of every female virtue...
and if success answer's the married couples fond
wishes and expectation, she will, in the true sense
of the word, be worth a great deal of money, and
consequently, a great fortune."*

To further explain why many historians believe Benjamin did
not include girls in his education plan, they look at the
written conversation Benjamin had with one of his female
friends, who talked of her interest in education.

*Benjamin stated, "...but there is nothing of equal
importance than being a good daughter, a good
wife, and a good mother."*

Simply, Benjamin did not understand women who wanted
more than what, he and many others of his time believed,
women needed. While he did believe that women should be
taught the basic functions and skills, which would be useful
to them and their families, such as writing, accounting, and
reading; he did not believe they needed to learn outside of
that box. And this educational belief was carried in his own
home. While his son, William, learned was involved in all
types of classes from geography to history to philosophy;
Sally learned how to embroider, knit, and spin.

On top of excluding girls from his formal schooling plan, Benjamin Franklin had a very clear vision of the school. He wanted it to be a comfortable, kind of home-like environment for the students. In his booklet describing the school, Benjamin stated the school should have a garden and a field. He also stated that the school should have a grand library, which should include not only books but maps, globes, and equipment for experiments. He also wanted swimming to be a focus of the school's curriculum, along with other forms of exercise. On top of explaining his plan for what should be taught at the school, he also discussed the conduct of the teachers. This was very important to Benjamin because, in one of his schools, he had a teacher that he did not get along with and it affected his grades. Once he was able to switch to a different teacher, one who he liked, he was one of the best students in his class. Benjamin said that the teachers at his school should be patient with a child's learning. He also stated they should set morals and be an example of these morals.

☙❧

After Benjamin released his booklet explaining the school, he set about raising funds, gathering individuals for a Board of Trustees, and oversaw construction. In 1751, the first school of its kind opened its doors to all boys who showed the ability to succeed at the school, no matter what their financial background was. The school was called the Philadelphia Academy, and Charitable School and attendance grew quickly. The school was renamed the University of Pennsylvania in 1779 when Pennsylvania's assembly gained control of the school.

☙❧

Along with a school, Benjamin Franklin also helped build a hospital in Philadelphia. While this was not originally Benjamin's idea, when Dr. Thomas Bond, who was having trouble with support and funding for a hospital, came to Franklin, Benjamin threw himself into the role. To raise support and money, Benjamin began to hold meetings, noted and wrote about the cause in his newspaper, and petitioned congress for funding. Thanks to the help from Benjamin Franklin, the Pennsylvania Hospital, which is still in operation, was founded in 1751. The hospital's first patient was admitted in 1752, but construction was not completed until three years later. Because of the humane treatment, the hospital not only provided to the physically ill but also mentally ill, the hospital grew rapidly. Soon the hospital had more patients than beds. By the time Benjamin Franklin passed away in 1790, there were two more wings and many more doctors.

❧ VII ❧

BENJAMIN FRANKLIN
AND THE AMERICAN
REVOLUTION

"All mankind is divided into three classes: those that are immovable, those that are movable, and those that move."

— BENJAMIN FRANKLIN

AN ENEMY OF BENJAMIN

❦

While Benjamin Franklin is known as a scientist, to many people, he is more well known as a Founding Father of the United States of America.

❦

Benjamin Franklin was generally known as a very generous and compassionate gentleman. He always tried to do good in the world and be the best person he could be. But, there were a few people Benjamin Franklin would grow to dislike and one of these men was King George III.

❦

While Benjamin supported King George III when he was crowned King in 1760, Benjamin started to feel that George did not genuinely care about his people. Benjamin felt King

George III especially did not care about the people's happiness in the American Colonies. By the time 1776 rolled around, Benjamin Franklin wanted nothing to do with King George III.

> Benjamin stated, "The King will stand foremost in the list of diabolical, bloody, and execrable tyrants."

NO TAXATION WITHOUT
REPRESENTATION

☙❧

W hile there were many steps which helped cause the American Revolution, one of the biggest ones was the Stamp Act of 1765. In attempts to raise money, the British Parliament passed this act to try to raise money so they could get out of debt. This act stated that many paper materials, such as newspaper, pamphlets, legal contracts, and wills included a special tax. On top of this, the tax could only be paid in gold or silver coins.

*Like many American Colonists, Benjamin Franklin
was outraged about the Stamp Act stating, "This
act is the mother of mischief."*

☙❧

With Benjamin living in London when the Stamp Act made its way throughout the colonies, a rumor was started that Benjamin and the Franklin family were supporters of the

Stamp Act. Through a letter from his wife, Deborah, Benjamin learned many colonists created a mob in front of the Franklin house.

> The letter to Benjamin from Deborah read, "I fetched a gun or two...we maid one room into a magazin. I ordered sum sorte of defen upstairs such as I could manaig my self."

This letter would also be an example of why Benjamin, at one time, felt the English alphabet could be improved as many women of the time spelled as badly as Deborah.

The news of a mob forming in front of his family's home not only disturbed Benjamin because he was concernedabout the safety of his family. It also bothered him because he knew these were not the American Colonists he had ones lived near and knew. For the change of behavior from the American Colonists, Benjamin began to blame the Stamp Act.

Because of the American Colonists reaction to the Stamp Act, British Parliament asked a few colonists, one being Benjamin Franklin, why the American Colonists felt the way they did about the Stamp Act. In his speech to the British Parliament, Benjamin asked and answered questions about the situation that he had rehearsed previously.

The first question Benjamin asked the British

Parliament was "Do you think the people of
America would submit to pay the stamp duty if it
was moderated?"
When he asked moderated, he was asking if the
British Parliament would limit or change the
Stamp Act. For his answer, Benjamin Franklin
stated, "No, never, unless compelled by force
of arms..."

Many historians believe that when Benjamin Franklin was speaking to the British Parliament about the Stamp Act, he was leading to the fact that American Colonists were leading towards independence from Great Britain due to some of the things he said, such as the American Colonists would only pay the Stamp Act if they had to due to losing a war.

૭ૐૐ

The second question and answer Benjamin Franklin
discussed when he met the British Parliament
was "What was the temper of American towards
Great Britain before the year 1763?" Benjamin's
answer to this question was "The best in the
world. They submitted willingly to the
government of the Crown...They had not only
respect, but an affection for Great Britain, for its
laws, its customs and manners, and even a
fondness for its fashions..." The third question
Benjamin asked the Parliament was "And how
was their temper now," and its answer was "Oh,
very much altered."

૭ૐૐ

According to one member of the British Parliament, they were all ears when Benjamin Franklin was asking and answering his own questions during the meeting. Today, some people wonder if, because of Benjamin's use of the words "their" if he was hinting that the American Revolution was approaching. However, no evidence cantruly support this reasoning.

❖

About a week after Benjamin Franklin spoke before the British Parliament, he received news that the Stamp Act had been repealed. "I am just no made very happy by vote...for the repeal of the Stamp Act."

Benjamin wrote after he had received the news. Many other American Colonists were also happy and gave Benjamin Franklin a lot of credit for getting the Stamp Act repealed. Once the news started to reach the American Colonies, they began to cheer for Benjamin and praised him for his work. However, much of the hard feelings from the American Colonists towards Great Britain would stick with them for many years to come.

❖

On the other side of the sea, the British were less excited about the repeal of the Stamp Act. As the American Colonists were cheering for Benjamin Franklin, the British newspapers were publishing cartoons which showed Benjamin Franklin in a bad light. They were angry that the Stamp Act had been repealed and continued to believe that American Colonists should pay for the British government's costs for printing all the stamps that were not worthless. When Benjamin Franklin heard about this, he was displeased at their anger towards the American Colonists. Just like many other American Colonists, Benjamin Franklin did not believe that the now worthless stamps, which had caused the British government so much money, were at the hands of the colonies. In response, Benjamin published a strange and slightly naughty story in the London newspaper.

A REVOLUTIONARY SONG

❧

Because of the way the British still felt towards the American Colonies after the Stamp Act was repealed, the colonies also started to feel anger towards their Mother Country. And these hard feelings did not help with Great Britain continued to try to pass acts on the colonies, without their consent.

❧

In 1767, the Townshend Acts were passed on the American Colonies by the British Parliament. The parliament was convinced that the American Colonies existed only because Great Britain supported them, especially financially. There-fore, they continued to try to add tax to certain goods in the colonies. The Townshend Acts were a series of acts that placed taxes on specific materials, such as paper, tea, and glass. In response, the American Colonists began to boycott the items that had been taxed. Benjamin Franklin approved of the boycotting as he felt that Britain had a bad attitude towards the colonies and wanted this attitude to change.

> *As Benjamin stated during that time, "...every man in this city seems to think himself a sovereign over America; seems to jostle himself into the throne with the king and talks of our subjects in the colonies."*

༺☙❧༻

With the Townshend Acts, the American Colonists continued to rise against the new taxes and other acts Great Britain was sending their way. In fact, the riots in the American Colonies got so bad that the British Parliament decided to send British soldiers to the colonies to try to stop the rioting. However, many American Colonists started to attack the British soldiers through insulting and teasing them. It was at this moment that Benjamin Franklin began to warn the British Parliament that they were pushing the American Colonists too far and they were taking a dangerous step sending troops to the colonies.

༺☙❧༻

In 1770, after all the backlash the American Colonists were giving the British Parliament, the Parliament finally decided to repeal all but one Townshend Act. The one act that remained was the tax on tea. It was then that the Colonists and British soldiers came to a head in Boston. On March 5th of that year, the British soldiers starting shooting at the unarmed American Colonists, at least the ones who came to throw snowballs at the British soldiers. Benjamin Franklin was heartbroken and angry when he read what the British soldiers did to the American Colonists in London. Franklin called the soldiers cowards for their actions.

❦

In 1773, the Tea Act was passed on the colonies by the British Parliament, which resulted in the Boston Tea Party. It was at this time that Benjamin Franklin realized that there would probably be no reconciliation between the American Colonies and their Mother Country.

> *Benjamin stated of the situation, "I am at a loss to see how peace and union are to be restored."*

❦

It was also at his time that Benjamin Franklin put a song to the feelings the American Colonists had towards Great Britain. The song was titled "We have an Old Mother" and had the following lyrics, which were sang to the tune of "Which Nobody Can Deny:"

> *We have an old mother that*
> *peevish is grown.*
> *She snubs us like children that*
> *scarce walk alone.*
> *She forgets we're grown up and*
> *have a sense of our own.*
> *Which nobody can deny, deny.*
> *Which nobody can deny.*
> *If we don't obey orders,*
> *whatever the case;*
> *She frowns and she chides,*
> *and she loses all patience,*

and sometimes she hits us
a slap in the face.
Which nobody can deny, deny.
Which nobody can deny.
Her order so odd are,
we often suspect
That age has impaired
her sound intellect.
But still an old mother
should have some respect.
Which nobody can deny, deny.
Which nobody can deny.
We'll join her in lawsuits
to baffle all those
Who, to get what she has,
will be often her foes;
But we know it must all be
our own, when she goes.
Which nobody can deny, deny.
Which nobody can deny.

༺✤༻

After the Boston Tea Party, the British Parliament passed the Coercive Acts, which the American Colonists began to call the Intolerable Acts. Because the British Parliament felt the American Colonists needed to be better controlled, they sent more British soldiers to the colonies. On top of this, they closed the Boston Harbor and suspended town meetings until the American Colonists repaid the tax on the tea.

With Benjamin Franklin still in London during this
time, he hears what the British citizens are saying
about the American Colonists, and it angers him.

*"I have heard the government condemn
Americans," Benjamin Franklin wrote, "as the
lowest of mankind, and almost of a different
species from the British of England. They heap
upon us both scorn, and contempt...in my mind
government should pay us for all the duties
extorted by armed forces."*

At this point, Benjamin Franklin felt and knew that war could easily be the next step for the American Colonists and he wanted to try to end this before any type of war started. Therefore, he requested to meet with the British Parliament but was turned down. Instead, the Privy Council, which was a group of nobles who would advise King George III, asked to see Benjamin Franklin in a meeting.

෴

The meeting between Benjamin Franklin and the Privy Council occurred at the beginning of 1774. During this whole meeting, the council took out all their anger towards the American Colonists on Benjamin Franklin, completely humiliating him in front of many British citizens. While it is said that Benjamin Franklin stood there like a rock the whole time, he let his anger towards Great Britain show after the meeting ended. He was walking beside the main council person who tormented him during the meeting.

*It was then Benjamin Franklin grabbed the man by
the arm and stated, "I will make your master a
little king for this."*

It was at this point Benjamin Franklin knew the war was to come as it could longer be pushed aside or denied.

BENJAMIN'S VARIOUS
REVOLUTIONARY TASKS

꧁꧂

I n 1775, Benjamin came back to the American Colonies, which was now at the start of the war. Less than 24 hours after being on American soil, Benjamin Franklin was appointed to the Second Continental Congress. Once Ben started to go to the meetings held by the congress, he soon realized that he was one of the few men who knew that the American Colonies had to fight for their independence. Because of this, Benjamin threw himself into doing whatever he could for the independent cause. These tasks would often keep him so busy while he was not sitting in his seat in the Continental Congress that he barely slept, and it began to show when he was in his seat. At one point, Founding Father and second President of the United States of America, John Adams said that Franklin was often "*fast asleep in his chair*" during Continental Congress debates.

꧁꧂

The tasks Benjamin did for the Revolutionary cause were varied. For almost two years, Benjamin raised funds and weapons for the army, organized the Pennsylvania militia, reviewed troops, drew up plans for Philadelphia's naval defense, and create a new mailing system. The British government still controlled the previous mailing system, so nothing was being delivered to the American Colonists. Therefore, Benjamin set up a system in various cities around the colonies.

❦

On top of all this, Benjamin was also part of the committee which was to draft the Declaration of Independence. While the task of writing the Declaration of Independence went to Thomas Jefferson, who became the third President of the United States of America, Benjamin did help with it. While Benjamin Franklin was getting over an illness, which had caused a nasty rash, Thomas Jefferson asked Benjamin Franklin to edit the finished draft of the Declaration of Independence. Benjamin mainly did minor editing, such as straightening phrases. However, there was one significant change the Benjamin Franklin made, which was changing Thomas Jefferson's "sacred and undeniable" to "self-evident."

> *Therefore, the statement then said, "...we hold these truths to be self-evident; that all men are created equal."*

❦

When the Second Continental Congress read and edited the draft of the Declaration of Independence, they were not as kind as Benjamin Franklin was. Throughout the whole process, Thomas Jefferson sat there as he watched and listen to members of the Second Continental Congress tear apart the draft. Benjamin Franklin could tell that this was not only embarrassing Thomas Jefferson but also saw he was becoming angry at the editing. In attempts to try to make Thomas Jefferson feel better about the situation, Benjamin Franklin told Thomas Jefferson a story. From this day on, Thomas Jefferson and Benjamin Franklin continued to be friends. Thomas Jefferson had high respect for Benjamin Franklin, especially for the help Franklin had given Jefferson during the writing of the Declaration of Independence. Jefferson also had a soft spot for Benjamin Franklin because of the kindness Franklin showed Jefferson when the rest of the Second Continental Congress was tearing apart his draft of the Declaration of Independence. In fact, Thomas Jefferson was one of the last friends to visit Benjamin Franklin before Franklin's passing. Thisget together took place in March of 1790. Jefferson went to visit Franklin in his home, and the two spent their day talking about the times they had and Jefferson mention that he was rather excited to hear about how Benjamin Franklin had been writing his autobiography.

> *Benjamin replied, "I cannot say much of that, but I will give you a sample of what I shall leave." When Jefferson promised to read it and then return it to Franklin as soon as he could, Franklin told Thomas Jefferson to keep the sample. Later in his life, Thomas Jefferson discussed how great this gift was that Benjamin Franklin had given him stating, "The venerable and beloved Franklin gave me handwritten pages of his life."*

The Second Continental Congress approved the Declaration of Independence on June 2, 1776, and all fifty-six Founding Fathers had signed the document on July 4, 1776.

> *Once the document was signed, Benjamin Franklin reportedly stated, "we must hang together, or most assuredly, we shall all hang separately."*

Benjamin, like all the other Founding Fathers, knew they were committing treason, which had a punishment of death. It was also on July 4, 1776, when the Declaration of Independence was read to the public in Pennsylvania's Statehouse Yard. The Declaration of Independence was printed and handed out to as many colonists as it could be. The colonists then started to tear down statues of King George III as they celebrated in joy. For Benjamin Franklin, declaring independence from the Mother Country meant that everything needed to be done at the same time. As much as possible needed to be completed as soon as possible. Just as many other Americans knew, and what every Founding Father knew, the newly formed United States of America would need to win that Revolutionary War, which had been going on for a little more than a year, if they really wanted to gain their independence.

❧ VIII ☙

BENJAMIN FRANKLIN'S LAST CHAPTER

"Our new Constitution is now established, everything seems to promise it will be durable; but, in this world, nothing is certain except death and taxes."

— BENJAMIN FRANKLIN

BENJAMIN FRANKLIN IS SENT
TO FRANCE

☙❧

A t the end of 1776, with the Revolutionary War still raging on, Benjamin Franklin said goodbye to Philadelphia. Even in his old age, he was tasked with traveling to France to gain support for the American cause. At the time, Benjamin felt he would never return to America, so it was a very solemn farewell to his family, friends, and the newly formed United States of America. Benjamin knew that this would not be an easy task, trying to get France to side with the United States of America, but he knew it was possible and Benjamin worked hard to gain the respect of France officials.

☙❧

Through his time in France, Benjamin heard of all the news about the Revolutionary War. He would hear of the victories which were won by the American forces and the battles which were lost by the American forces. Throughout this time, Benjamin tried not to let the losses distract him from his mission in France. However, this was especially difficult when Benjamin Franklin received the news that the British had captured Philadelphia. This was where his family was located. This was the city that Benjamin Franklin's daughter, Sally, her husband, and her children lived. Benjamin was devastated and worried about this news. But when the news broke in November of 1777, Benjamin was at the height of trying to get France onto the side of the United States of America. Of course, for France, this only escalated their feelings that the United States of America could not survive without Great Britain. However, for Benjamin Franklin, it just put a brighter fire in him to accomplish his task so he could help make sure that the United States of America would win the war and indeed gain their independence. By this point, it meant not only saving his life, and the lives of all the other fifty-five Founding Fathers, but also the life of his family.

৩৶৩

It was only a month later from the news that the British troops had taken of Philadelphia when the French realized that the United States of America would make a good ally for them. It was in December of 1777 when word spread to Benjamin and France that the whole British Army were prisoners of war. That following year, on February 6, 1778, the Treaty of Alliance was signed. This marked that France had finally joined the United States of America in their fight for independence. At the same time, King Louis XVI began to not only see the United States of America as an independent country but also saw Benjamin Franklin as the country's ambassador. Therefore, instead of heading home to the United States of American after the treaty was signed,

Benjamin Franklin remained in France as the United States of America's ambassador.

※

It was not until after the Treaty of Alliance was signed that France started to learn the actual state of the American Revolution and the soldiers fighting it when Benjamin Franklin started to become involved in military planning with France. While others were looking into shipping French soldiers off to America, Benjamin Franklin was looking at sending some to England. Benjamin started working with John Paul Jones, who was an American Navy Captain. The first thing they did was get Jones and his crew a bigger ship to sail towards England. Benjamin then gave Jones a strict order to watch the British prisoners. Benjamin told Jones that his men were not to hurt any of the men.

> *He also told Jones, "...though the English have wantonly burned many defenseless towns in America, you are not to follow their example."*

While Jones and his crew were sailing to England, they encountered Serapis, the British ship which was on its way to America. Jones, his crew, and the British on the Serapis engaged in battle on September 3, 1779, with Jones ending the battle by capturing the Serapis. With the news of the capture, both France and America gave joyous praise. Not only was this an American victory but it was a victory which was won in England's sea.

※

With the British General Charles Cornwallis surrendering

the British army to George Washington in October of 1781 in the Battle of Yorktown, the American Revolutionary War was over, and America had fully gained its independence. However, a peace treaty still needed to be negotiated between The United States of America and England. Therefore, Congress chose John Jay, John Adams, Benjamin Franklin, Henry Laurens, and Temple Franklin, who was Benjamin's grandson as the American Peace Commission to negotiate the treaty. However, the negotiations would go on for a couple of years and came very close to ending a few times. At first, England offered America limited independence, but the men refused. They wanted England to pay for some of the cost of the war, England refused. It was not until near the end of 1783 that a peace treaty was negotiated and signed. England agreed to pay for all the towns and homes they had destroyed if the United States of America would pay for the businesses and homes they seized from loyalists. England also recognized the United States of America's full independence and maintained peace with the newly formed independent country. The Peace Treaty was signed by John Adams, John Jay, and Benjamin Franklin on behalf of the United States of America. On the side of England, the treaty was signed by David Harley, who was a member of the Parliament.

> *It was at this moment that Benjamin Franklin truly felt the war for independence was over, and he celebrated with joy, writing to a friend, "We are now friends with England and with all mankind. May we never see another war! For, in my opinion, there was never a good war or a bad peace."*

BENJAMIN FRANKLIN'S LAST
RETURN HOME

❧

In July of 1785, Benjamin Franklin retired from his ambassador position and decided to live out his remaining years with his family in Philadelphia. Benjamin stepped foot on American soil in September of 1785 to a joyous welcome. Benjamin was elected the sixth President of the Supreme Executive Council of Pennsylvania on October 18, 1785. A position he held until October 31, 1787. For the rest of his life, Benjamin laid low, mainly due to illness. He was often bedridden, even during his time as President of the Supreme Executive Council of Pennsylvania. After telling his daughter, Sally, that he was ready to go to his eternal home after she begged him to stay, Benjamin Franklin passed away on April 17, 1790.

❧ IX ❧
EPILOGUE

❦

Throughout his life, Benjamin Franklin was a man before his time. He was also a man who never gave himself as much credit as he deserved. Even with his fame and fortune, he never stopped trying to do good every day and be the best person he could be. But this is only one of the legacies Benjamin Franklin has left behind. Even today, Benjamin Franklin is considered one of the most prominent Colonial Americans not only of his time but throughout the history of Colonial America. Many feel that Benjamin Franklin is the real father of the United States of America. This is because he was the only one of the Founding Fathers who sighed all four documents so that the United States of America could truly claim its independence from the Mother Country. These documents were: The Declaration of Independence, the Treaty of Alliance, the Treaty of Paris, and the Constitution of the United States.

༄༅

Benjamin Franklin has many strengths that helped him become such an iconic figure in American history. A few of these strengths were intelligence, determination, compassion, understanding, and hard work. Often, Benjamin would mix these strengths together to make his goal of becoming the best person he could be. For example, being able to help negotiate not one but two peace treaties would have used the strengths of intelligence, determination, and understanding at least. Today, we can learn from Benjamin Franklin's strengths in many ways. One of the most significant ways we can learn from Franklin is simply to ask ourselves the same question he asked himself every morning: What good can I do today? Like many countries in the world today, Benjamin Franklin lived in an ever-changing world and not only lived through the American Revolution, which is one of America's bloodiest wars but also was a grand part of the American Revolution and the fight for independence. He was able to use all his strengths to create a better world not only for himself and his family but for most people in the United States of America. As Benjamin felt in his life, people deserved to be treated with respect and compassion. They deserved to be understood. And this is very true today. All people deserve to be treated with respect, understanding, and compassion.

༄༅

Of course, like every human, Benjamin Franklin is just that: human. Therefore, with all his great strengths he also has weaknesses. While a man of his time, one of his weaknesses was not spreading his understanding and compassion to all human life. While he believed women were not to be harmed, he also believed they were not capable of the same education as a male. Furthermore, for part of his life, Benjamin Franklin supported the institution as slavery and never saw African Americans as equals. However, near the end of his life, Benjamin did petition Congress to end slavery, he still did not truly believe in equality. Another weakness of Benjamin Franklin was forgiveness and anger. When it came to his oldest son, William, siding with England during the American Revolution, Benjamin Franklin never forgave his child. While he still loved his son, their relationship was never restored after the American Revolution because Benjamin Franklin simply could not let go of the anger he held towards William to truly forgive him. We can learn from Franklin's weaknesses by being able to let go of our anger and forgive others who have hurt us at any points in our lives.

❧ X ❧
AFTERWORD

❦

This book is only a piece of the history of Benjamin Franklin, his legacy, and the times Benjamin Franklin lived in. Historians have been studying and writing about Benjamin Franklin for decades and, as a result, there are dozens of excellent books about Benjamin Franklin.

❦

The first book is titled, *The First American: The Life and Times of Benjamin Franklin*. This book was written by H.W. Brands and published in 2002.

❦

The second book is titled, *Benjamin Franklin, An American Life*.

The author of this book is Walter Isaacson and was published in 2004.

❦

The third book is *The Autobiography of Benjamin Franklin*, which was written by Franklin himself and has been published numerous times.

❧ XI ❧
ACKNOWLEDGMENTS

❀

Beeman, Richard R. "Benjamin Franklin and the American Enlightenment." In The Autobiography of Benjamin Franklin: Penn Reading Project Edition edited by Conn Peter, by Franklin Benjamin and Gutmann Amy, 145-49. Philadelphia: University of Pennsylvania Press, 2005.

❀

"Benjamin Franklin." Biography.com. August 02, 2017. Accessed June 05, 2018.

❀

"Benjamin Franklin Quotes (Author of The Autobiography of Benjamin Franklin)." Goodreads. Accessed June 14, 2018.

Brands, H. W. *The First American: The Life and times of Benjamin Franklin*. Norwalk, CT.: Easton Press, 2002.

Franklin, Benjamin, and Alfred H. Tamarin. *Benjamin Franklin; an AutobiographicalPortrait*. London: Collier-Macmillan, 1969.

Franklin, Benjamin. *The Benjamin Franklin Papers*. New York: Dodd, Mead & Company, 1962.

Franklin, Benjamin. "Unpublished Letters of Benjamin Franklin." The Pennsylvania Magazine of History and Biography 15, no. 1 (1891): 35-40.

Hornberger, Theodore. "Benjamin Franklin." In Benjamin Franklin - American Writers 19: University of Minnesota Pamphlets on American Writers, 5-45. MINNEAPOLIS: University of Minnesota Press, 1962.

Isaacson, Walter. *Benjamin Franklin: An American Life*. New York: Simon & Schuster, 2006.

Seeger, Raymond J. "Benjamin Franklin, American Physicist." Journal of the Washington Academy of Sciences 66, no. 2 (1976): 139-46.

"The Autobiography of Benjamin Franklin." In The Autobiography of Benjamin Franklin: Penn Reading Project Edition, edited by Goodman Nathan G. and Conn Peter, by Franklin Benjamin and Gutmann Amy, 7-142. Philadelphia: University of Pennsylvania Press, 2005.

Ward, John William. "Who Was Benjamin Franklin?" The American Scholar 32, no. 4 (1963): 541-53.

Wood, Gordon S. *The Americanization of Benjamin Franklin*. London: Penguin Books, 2005.

YOUR FREE EBOOK!

As a way of saying thank you for reading our book, we're offering you a free copy of the below eBook.

Happy Reading!

Made in the USA
Las Vegas, NV
11 June 2022